SCHAU
POP FAVORITES

ARRANGED BY WESLEY SCHAUM

CONTENTS

Art: Christine Pruett
Editor: Carole Flatau

© 1995 BELWIN MILLS PUBLISHING CORP. (ASCAP)
All Rights Assigned to and Controlled by Alfred Publishing Co., Inc.
All Rights Reserved including Public Performance. Printed in USA.

From the Lucasfilm Ltd. Production - A Twentieth Century Fox Release "Star Wars"

Star Wars
(Main Title)

Music by JOHN WILLIAMS
Arranged by WESLEY SCHAUM

3

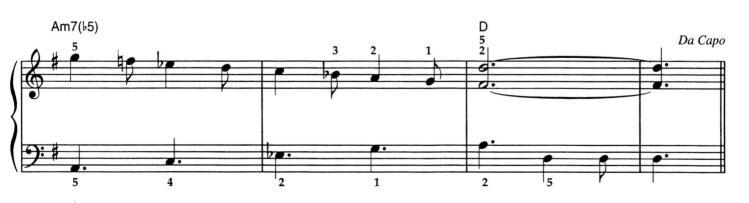

EL9529

Evergreen

Words by PAUL WILLIAMS

Music by BARBRA STREISAND
Arranged by WESLEY SCHAUM

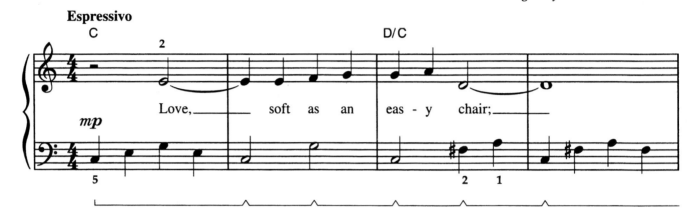

Love,_____ soft as an eas - y chair;_____

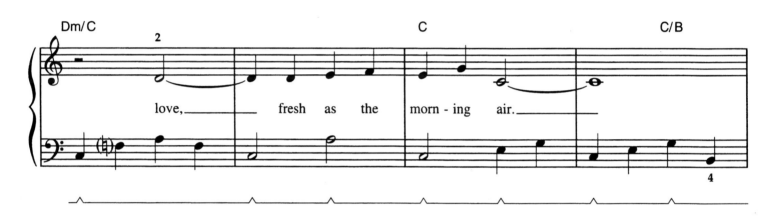

love,_____ fresh as the morn - ing air. _____

One_____ love that is shared by two,_____

I have found_____ with you. _____ Like a

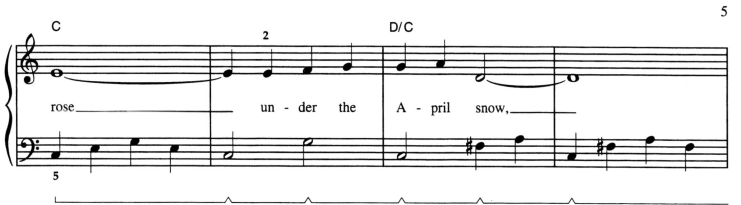

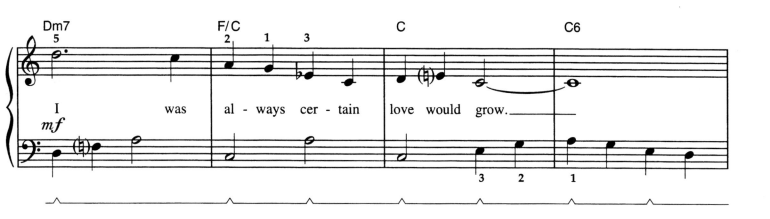

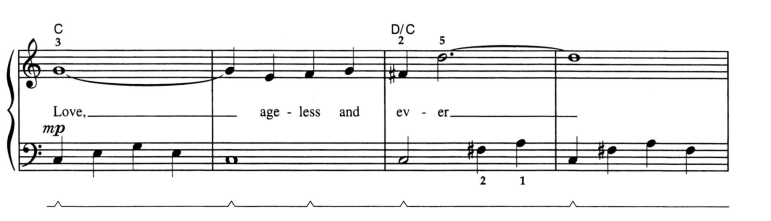

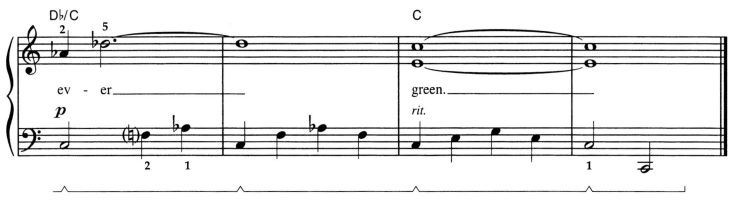

Begin the Beguine

Words and Music by COLE PORTER
Arranged by WESLEY SCHAUM

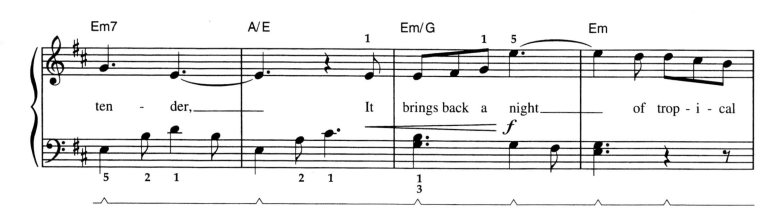

'S Wonderful

Music and Lyrics by
GEORGE GERSHWIN and IRA GERSHWIN
Arranged by WESLEY SCHAUM

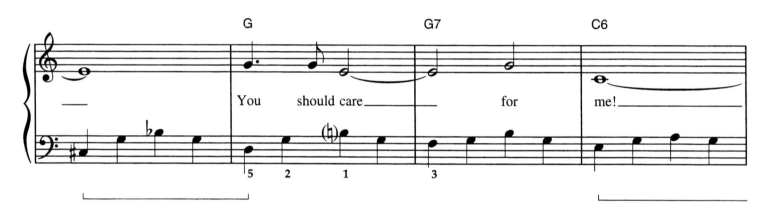

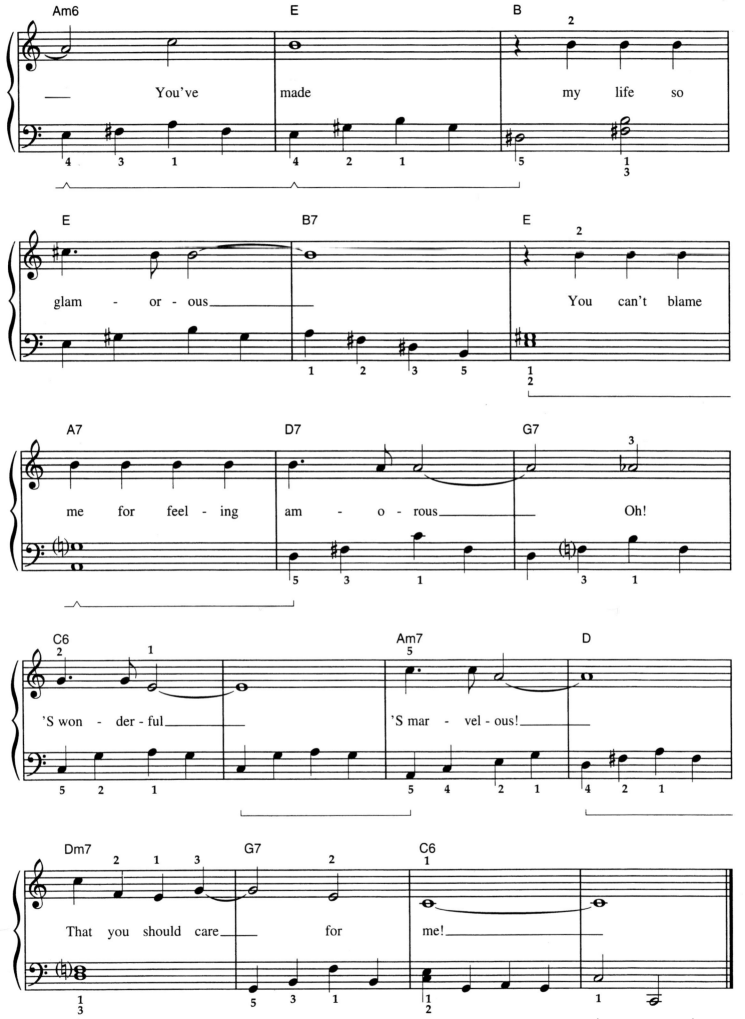

Theme From "A Summer Place"

Words by MACK DISCANT

Music by MAX STEINER
Arranged by WESLEY SCHAUM

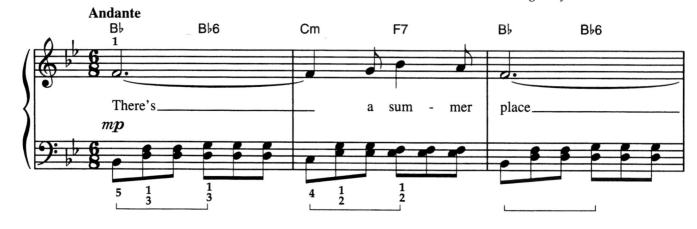

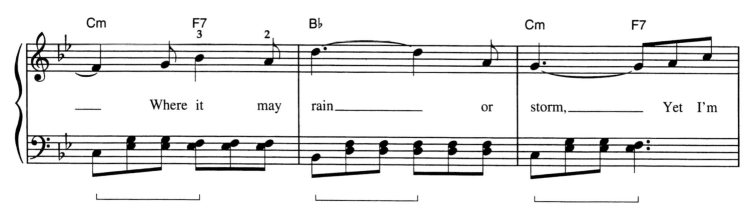

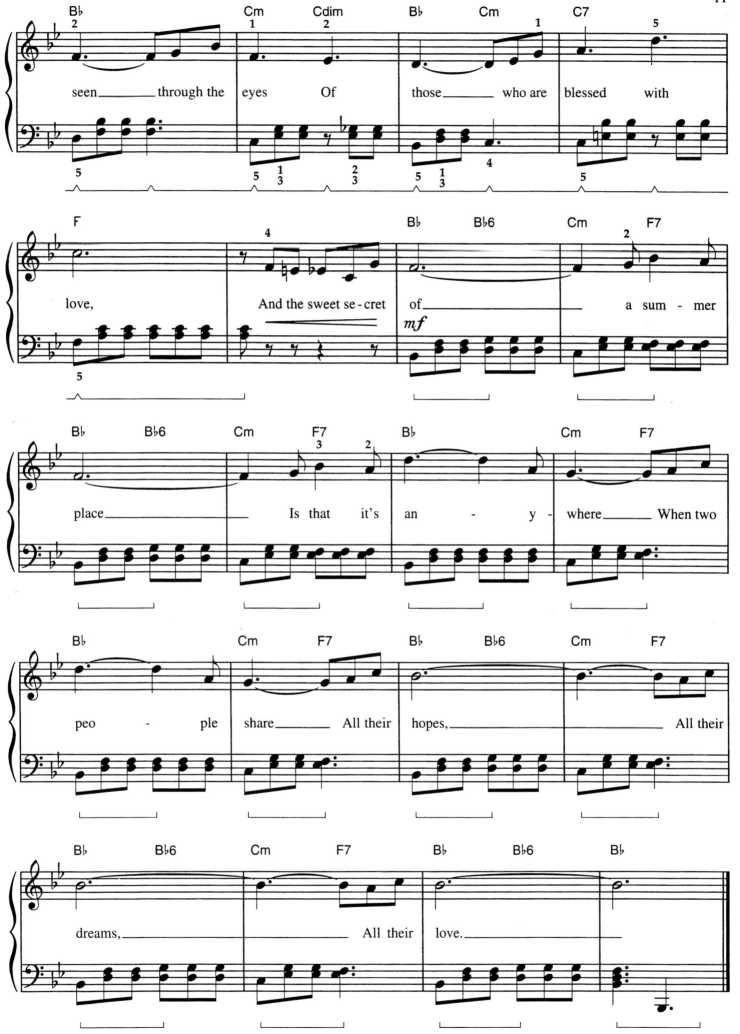

EL9529

12

Tea for Two

Words by IRVING CAESAR

Music by VINCENT YOUMANS
Arranged by WESLEY SCHAUM

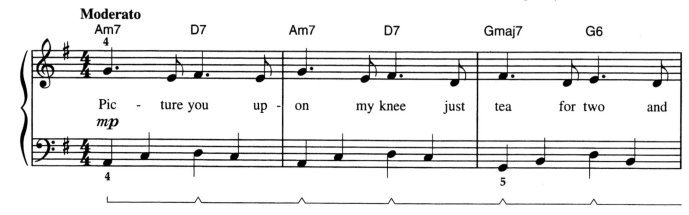

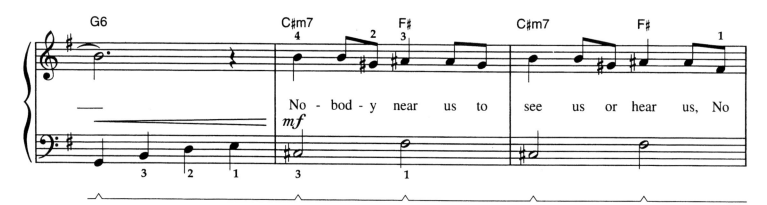

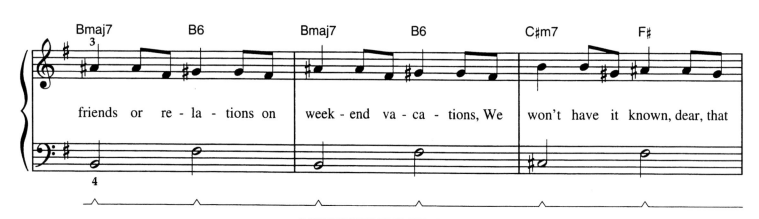

The Wind Beneath My Wings

Words and Music by
LARRY HENLEY and JEFF SILBAR
Arranged by WESLEY SCHAUM

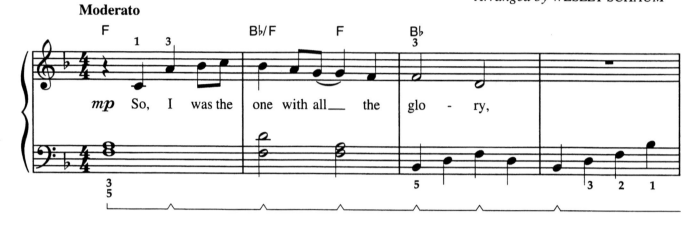

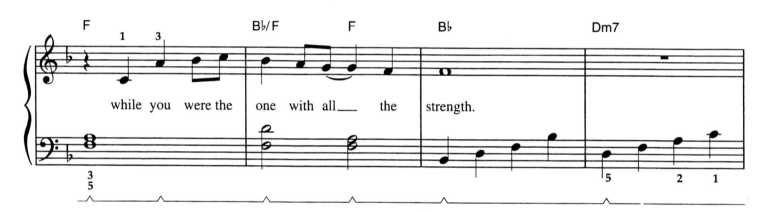

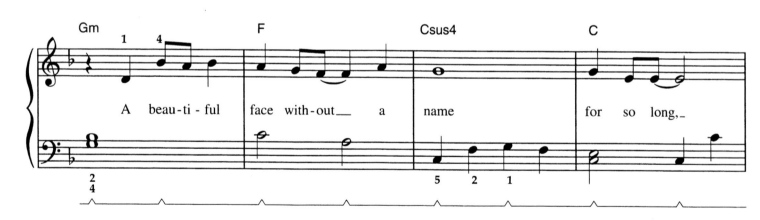

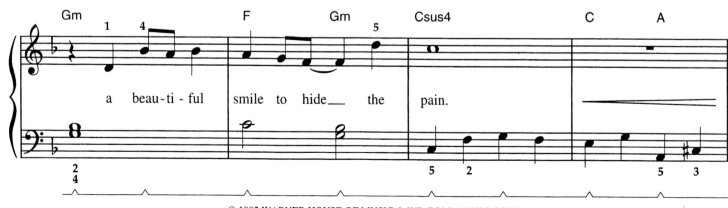

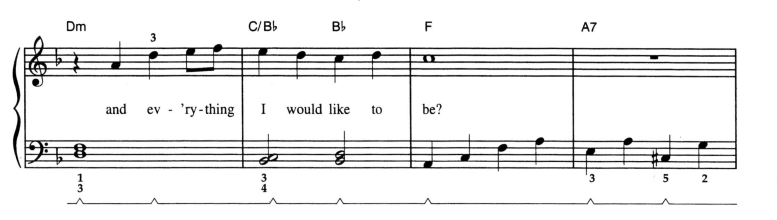

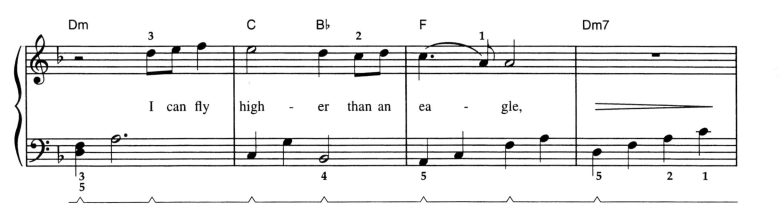

EL9529

From the Warner Bros. T.V. Movie "The Thorn Birds"

The Thorn Birds
(Main Theme)

By HENRY MANCINI
Arranged by WESLEY SCHAUM

Andantino

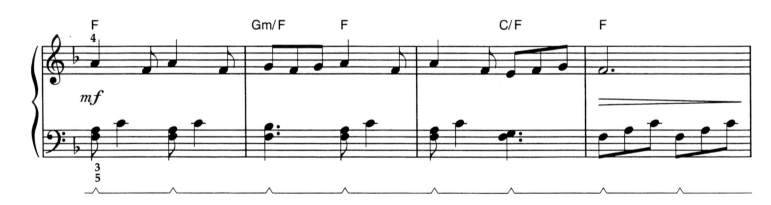

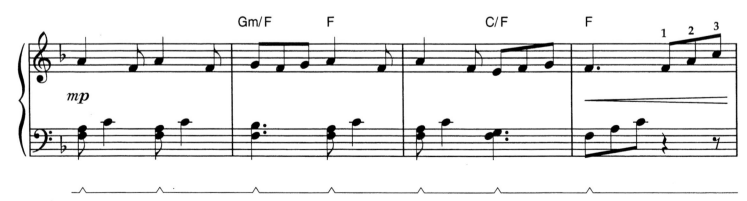

EL9529

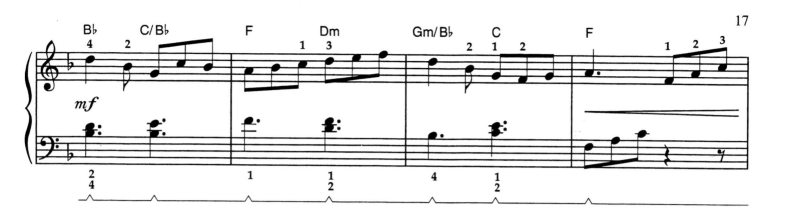

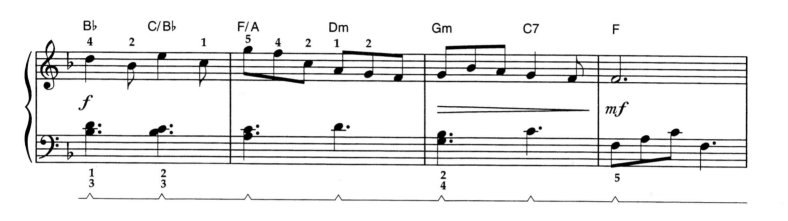

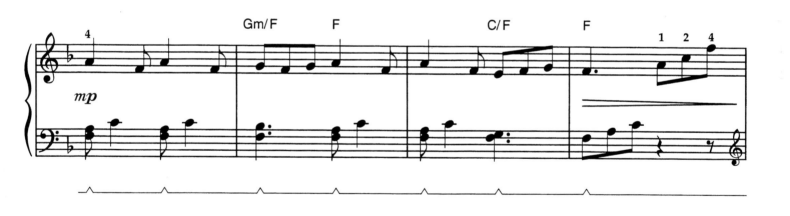

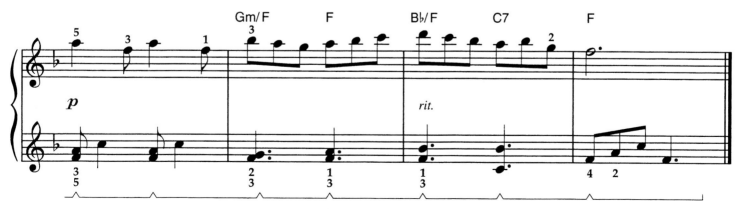

EL9529

Your Smiling Face

Words and Music by JAMES TAYLOR
Arranged by WESLEY SCHAUM

EL9529

I Only Have Eyes for You

Words by AL DUBIN

Music by HARRY WARREN
Arranged by WESLEY SCHAUM

Are the stars out to-night? I don't know if it's cloud-y or bright 'Cause I on-ly have eyes for you, dear. The moon may be high, but I can't see a thing in the sky, 'Cause I on-ly have eyes for you I don't know if we're in a

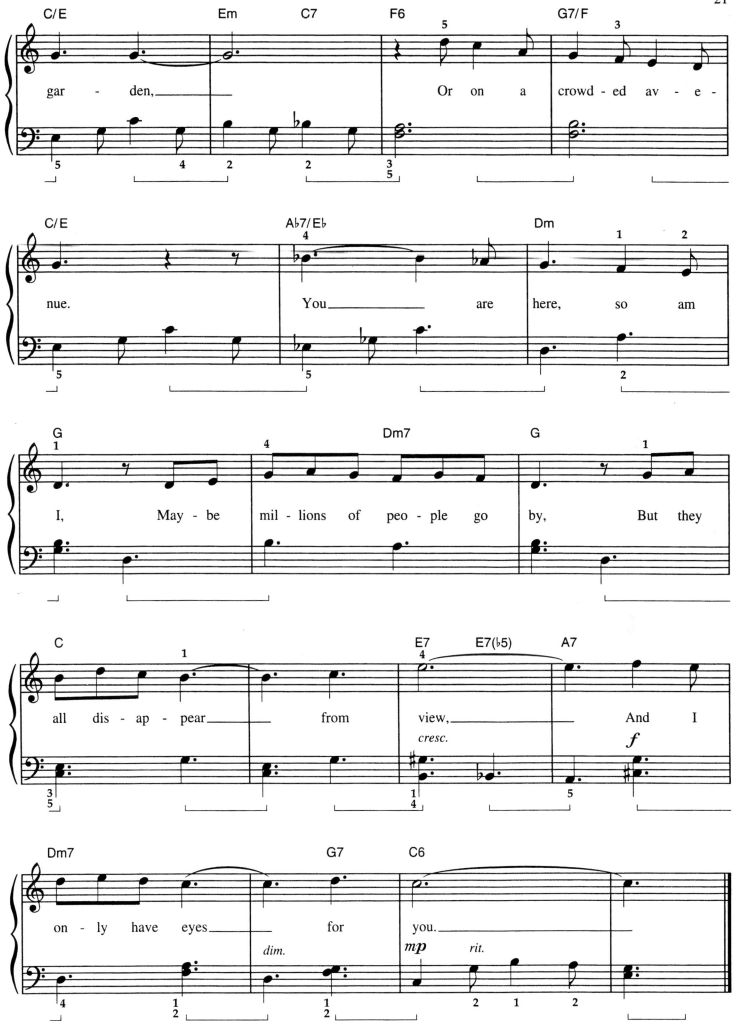

Featured in the M-G-M Picture "THE WIZARD OF OZ"

We're Off to See the Wizard

Words by
E.Y. HARBURG

Music by
HAROLD ARLEN
Arranged by WESLEY SCHAUM